GIVE YOURSELF A
GOLD STAR!

A JOURNAL OF EVERYDAY ACHIEVEMENTS

by Leslie Jonath

CHRONICLE BOOKS

SAN FRANCISCO

"We are all made of star stuff."

—CARL SAGAN

INTRODUCTION

"You get to a certain age and you feel the need to reward yourself for just existing."

—RUFUS WAINWRIGHT

When you were little did you ever get a Gold Star? It might have been a sticker on a spelling test or art project. Do you remember how that glinting star made you feel? It made you feel that you were a star.

For many people, a Gold Star is a pure form of recognition. While we think we have outgrown the need for this kind of validation, having that little extra seal of approval feels great! As much as any inspirational tool, getting a gold star can provide motivation toward goals both large and small (or at least help us get through the day with more kindness and humor).

Most people still look for these Gold Stars from the outside but learning how to give them from within can lead to a healthier, happier, more satisfied life. Gold Stars abound in the universe and there are many reasons to give them!

While we might think praise is reserved for big accomplishments like inventing an emission-free, alternate energy source or climbing Mount Everest naked, it's important to reward the small actions and moments each day—the little attainable achievements.

Maybe the world's problems can't be solved right away, but we can start with picking up one piece of litter, folding the laundry, or noticing a cool cloud in the sky. Teddy Roosevelt once said, "Do what you can with what you have where you are." Big goals start with little steps that can be done right now. Let's give Gold Stars for celebrating life, for the things we can do, to the people we know! The answer is not always to do more but to appreciate the things we do.

Give Yourself a Gold Star! will help you recognize that everyday is an opportunity to do something meaningful for ourselves, each other, and the planet.

A Universe of Reasons to Give Gold Stars

There are an infinite number of reasons to give Gold Stars, from accomplishing small daily tasks, to celebrating the joys of life, to reaching a lifetime goal. Your actual actions and goals will be specific to you, but living a Gold Star life means giving yourself as many Gold Stars as possible each day.

Astronomers estimate the universe contains more than one septillion stars, so there are plenty of stars for all. **Now it's time for you to give yourself some Gold Stars!**

DAILY STARS

———

"What is the good of the stars
and the trees, your sunrise
and the wind, if they do not
enter into our daily lives?"

—E.M. FORSTER

You may not realize it, but you already do all kinds of Gold Star things. Even the simplest tasks merit stars. Give yourself credit for the achievements that you take for granted. Some days it's enough to do one small thing (and most times doing a small thing leads to bigger things). Some of our greatest satisfaction comes from completing the little stuff. Folding laundry, flossing, washing dishes, vacuuming . . . the more mundane, the merrier.

Did You...

 Get out of bed on time? Gold Star!

 Take the stairs instead of an elevator? Gold Star!

 Drink an extra glass of water? Gold Star!

 Clear away some clutter? (Okay, one piece of clutter?) Gold Star!

 Floss your teeth? Gold Star!

 Spend five minutes reading something interesting? Gold Star!

Take a brisk walk or perhaps a slow saunter?
Gold Star!

 Think about the laundry? Gold Star!

 Actually do it? Two stars!

 Iron or fold it? Three stars!

 **Do the best you could today?
Gold Star!**

Write down a list of five to ten simple tasks you do daily—from feeding the cat to brushing your teeth. Give yourself a Gold Star for writing the list! Now give yourself a Gold Star for doing each one!

☆ 1.

☆ 2.

☆ 3.

☆ 4.

☆ 5.

☆ 6.

☆ 7.

☆ 8.

☆ 9.

☆ 10.

"The good news is that the moment you decide that what you know is more important than what you have been taught to believe, you will have shifted gears in your quest for abundance. Success comes from within, not from without."

— RALPH WALDO EMERSON

Keep a Did List

Instead of starting the day with a To-Do list, end the day by making a list of what you did! At the end of each day, write down what you accomplished, even the tiniest actions. Make the list as finely detailed as possible, with extra stars for starting things, taking next steps, almost finishing things, getting close to finishing things, and even writing the list itself.

What are some small things you did recently that made you happy?
Make a list, and see what you can do daily. Give yourself Gold Stars
each time you make one happen!

☆

☆

☆

☆

☆

☆

☆

☆

☆

What were today's smallest Gold Star moments?

Do you have some kind words to say to someone when they finish a simple task? Write some of these affirmations and say them to yourself each time you finish a task. Gold Star!

"You yourself, as much as anybody else in the entire universe, deserve your love and affection."

—GAUTAMA BUDDHA

What is on your Did List?

☆

☆

☆

☆

☆

☆

☆

☆

☆

☆

Did you learn anything new today?

SMALL STEPS STARS

"The journey of a thousand miles
begins with one step."

—LAO TZU

Maybe you have a big, big, big goal or something that feels big. How do you start and how do you stay motivated on that long journey? You break up that goal into small steps and give yourself a Gold Star for achieving each one. Every big goal has within it the opportunity for infinite stars, depending on how small and achievable you make the steps. Make them ridiculous! You can even give yourself a Gold Star for writing up the steps.

"Great things are not done by impulse but by a small series of things brought together."

—VINCENT VAN GOGH

Do you want to...

Run a marathon?

Step 1: Start with a walk around the block.

Step 2: Take a trot around the park.

Step 3: Join a running team and map out your training routine.

Write a book?

Step 1: Start with writing one paragraph.

Step 2: Write a whole page. Okay, write another paragraph.

Step 3: Repeat steps one and two until you have a chapter.

Step 4: Keep going until you have a rough draft.

Learn how to bake?

Step 1: Write down the name of someone you know who is a great baker and ask him or her to teach you one recipe.

Step 2: Select a few easy recipes and give them a go.

Step 3: Bake a cake for a friend.

Extra credit: Decorate your cake!

What is your big goal?

Write down a big goal. Now write down smaller steps necessary to get to that big goal. Break each step into even easier steps. How low can you go? Give yourself a Gold Star for just doing that. Now take the first teeny tiny step. Gold Star! Repeat.

☆ Big Goal: _____

Small Steps:

☆ _____

☆ _____

How Low Can I Go?
Smaller and Smaller Steps!

☆ _____

☆ _____

☆ _____

☆ _____

☆ _____

☆ _____

☆ Big Goal:
_____

Small Steps:

☆ _____

☆ _____

☆ _____

☆ _____

How Low Can I Go?
Smaller and Smaller Steps!

☆ _____

☆ _____

☆ _____

☆ _____

☆ _____

☆ _____

 Big Goal: _____

Small Steps:

☆ _____

☆ _____

☆ _____

☆ _____

How Low Can I Go?
Smaller and Smaller Steps!

☆ _____

☆ _____

☆ _____

☆ _____

☆ _____

☆ _____

☆ **Big Goal:**
_____

Small Steps:

☆ _____

☆ _____

☆ _____

☆ _____

How Low Can I Go?
Smaller and Smaller Steps!

☆ _____

☆ _____

☆ _____

☆ _____

☆ _____

☆ _____

☆ Big Goal: _____

Small Steps:

☆ _____

☆ _____

☆ _____

☆ _____

How Low Can I Go?
Smaller and Smaller Steps!

☆ _____

☆ _____

☆ _____

☆ _____

☆ _____

☆ _____

☆ Big Goal: _____

Small Steps:

☆ _____

☆ _____

☆ _____

☆ _____

How Low Can I Go?
Smaller and Smaller Steps!

☆ _____

☆ _____

☆ _____

☆ _____

☆ _____

☆ _____

"I believe a leaf of grass is no less than the journey-work of the stars."

—WALT WHITMAN

"Optimism is the faith that leads to achievement. Nothing can be done without hope and confidence."

—HELLEN KELLER

Conventional wisdom says you have to
start with the hardest task first,
but this can lead to amazing amounts of procrastination.

So try starting with the easiest task. Gaining easy stars

will give you super-giant momentum!

Write down the three biggest reasons you want to accomplish your big goal (Gold Star!). Now put those reasons somewhere you can look at them daily. Take one small step each day toward your goal.

1. _____

2. _____

3. _____

"Success is not final,
failure is not fatal:
it is the courage to
continue that counts."

—WINSTON CHURCHILL

Are you stuck?

Call a friend or mentor to help brainstorm one action step. Take that step. Give yourself a Gold Star for reaching out and taking action.

Keep going.

"Our greatest weakness lies in giving up. The most certain way to succeed is always to try just one more time."

—THOMAS EDISON

Use a calendar to note dates for all the mini goals. Break your goal into a schedule with dates attached. Give yourself mini deadlines. What can you do in a month? A week? A day? In this moment?

Date	Daily Goals	Star

Date	Weekly Goals	Star

Date	Monthly Goals	Star

Date	Daily Goals	Star

Date	Weekly Goals	Star

Date	Monthly Goals	Star

Date	Daily Goals	Star

Date	Weekly Goals	Star

Date	Monthly Goals	Star

"Satisfaction lies in the effort, not in the attainment. Full effort is victory."

—MAHATMA GANDHI

THINGS-YOU-HAVE-
BEEN-MEANING-TO-
DO-FOREVER STARS

"Perfect is the enemy of good."

—VOLTAIRE

How many things have been on your list since you can't even remember? And what about the things we all dread—like doing taxes, going to the DMV, making a doctor's appointment, revising a résumé, or cleaning the parrot's cage? Finally check them off the list and feel great!

Clean out the refrigerator or mow the lawn? Toss out that moldy cheese and crank up the lawn mower. Gold Star!

 Make an appointment to see the dentist/horse veterinarian/karma doctor? Pick up that phone/write that e-mail/send a telepathic message, and set it up. Gold Star!

 Tidy up? Start with putting things in piles. Gold Star!

 Now move those piles around, even if they just go from one table to another. Now put each pile away and give yourself a Gold Star for each one.

Start a recycling program for your neighborhood? Gold Star!

 Pay that parking ticket? Gold Star!

 Do some household accounting, finish an expense report, or conduct a piggy bank audit? Gold Star!

 Have a conversation with someone about something awkward or difficult? Make that call. Gold Star!

Write a list of three to five things you have been putting off the longest. (Give yourself a Gold Star for writing that list!) For each thing you don't want to do, pick one of those things and write down three tiny steps (Gold Star!). Now go take that first tiny step. Gold Star!

1.

2.

3.

4.

5.

☆ Did you write the list?

Tiny Steps:

1. _____

2. _____

3. _____

Tiny Steps:

1. _____

2. _____

3. _____

★

Are you afraid to start something?

Set a timer for ten minutes and start.

(You can do anything for ten minutes.)

Gold Star!

"And still, after all this
time, the Sun has never
said to the Earth,
'You owe me.'
Look what happens
with love like that.
It lights up the sky."

—HAFEZ

Practice productive avoidance.

If you don't want to do something, do something else

that is on your list and give yourself a Gold Star for that!

Productive avoidance stars

Didn't want to:
_____

☆ Instead did:
_____

Didn't want to:
_____

☆ Instead did:
_____

Didn't want to:
_____

☆ Instead did:
_____

Didn't want to:
_____

☆ Instead did:
_____

Didn't want to:
_____

☆ Instead did:
_____

★ **Reframe the thing you dread** into something pleasant. Need to go to the DMV? Think about what great people-watching you can do there. Dread raking leaves? What a great opportunity to get exercise and fresh air. Now tackle those tasks and give yourself GOLD STARS!

☆ _____

☆ _____

☆ _____

☆ _____

☆ _____

☆ _____

☆ _____

☆ _____

☆ _____

"The most effective way
to do it, is to do it."

—AMELIA EARHART

Did you do something productive today?

"Do one thing every day
that scares you."

—ELEANOR ROOSEVELT

THINGS-YOU-DIDN'T-DO-THAT-YOU-ARE-GLAD-YOU-DIDN'T-DO STARS

"When you get to the end of your rope, tie a knot and hang on."

—FRANKLIN D. ROOSEVELT

Didn't burn down the house? Didn't eat that chocolate fudge cupcake? Didn't lose your keys? Didn't take the wrong turn the wrong way on a one-way street? Sometimes the things we didn't do are as important as the things we did do. What small catastrophes did you avoid today? Give yourself a Gold Star for not causing a disaster!

Did You Successfully...

 Not eat that last piece of cake? Give yourself a Gold Star!

 Avoid locking yourself out of the house? Gold Star! If you did lock yourself out but remembered where you hid a spare key, Gold Star for that!

 Not leave your umbrella at home/on the bus? Gold Star!

 Not overcook the pot roast? Gold Star!

Not forget your anniversary, dog's birthday, or astrology appointment? Gold Star!

 Avoid oversleeping and missing an important meeting? Triple Gold Star!

 Not wear the tiger suit to that party you thought was a costume party but wasn't? Gold Star!

Write about all the great things that happened because you didn't do what you didn't want to do. Didn't forget to write that birthday card to your mom? Think about how happy she was. Didn't forget to book your tickets for your vacation? Write about how excited you are to go on your trip.

"You need chaos in your soul to give birth to a dancing star."

—FRIEDRICH NIETZSCHE

If you are trying not to do something, keep a "Didn't List"!

"We are all in the gutter
but some of us are
looking at the stars."

—OSCAR WILDE

Keep a list of go-to actions. Give yourself a Gold Star each time you replaced an old behavior with a new productive one.

Instead of _____ ,

I _____ .

Instead of _____ ,

I _____ .

Instead of _____ ,

I _____ .

Instead of _____ ,

I _____ .

Instead of _____ ,

I _____ .

Instead of _____ ,

I _____ .

Instead of _____ ,

I _____ .

Instead of _____ ,

I _____ .

Instead of _____ ,

I _____ .

Instead of _____ ,

I _____ .

Instead of _____ ,

I _____ .

Instead of _____ ,

I _____ .

★ **Take a few** moments each day to relax and recharge and reflect.

When you can't think of the right action to take, take a step back. Write down what you think and how you feel about the situation. It is okay to do nothing.

CELEBRATE EVERYTHING STARS!

"Dwell on the beauty of life.
Watch the stars, and see yourself
running with them . . ."

—MARCUS AURELIUS

There are so many reasons to celebrate!

Look around and see ways that you can more fully appreciate all the good things in life. Did you notice how blue the sky was? Order a new book? Plant a garden? Say something nice to a stranger? These are the fun things we do that are just cool—things that are off our "normal" path that expand our sense of what we can do and be.

Did you take the time to...

 Stop and smell the roses? Gold Star!

 Create something? A pie, a sandcastle, a silly poem? Gold Star!

 Throw a party for someone? Make them queen or king for a day? Gold Star!

 Look up at the night sky and appreciate all the stars? Gold Star!

 Write a thank-you card to someone for a gift they gave you long ago? Gold Star!

 Remember a time when a friend made you laugh? Write or call them and share that memory. Gold Star!

 Learn a fun fact about the universe, the moon and stars, or a foreign country and share it with someone? Gold Star!

 Try something new, like a new food, vocabulary word, or hairdo? Gold Star, Gold Star, and Gold Star!

 Run backward on the beach with your eyes closed? Gold Star!

 Use a flashlight to host a shadow puppet show? Gold Star!

Celebration stars are about gratitude. Write a list of the things and the people in life that you are grateful for and celebrate at least one each day with a Gold Star!

☆ _____

☆ _____

☆ _____

☆ _____

☆ _____

☆ _____

Are there any places in your city or town that you've always wanted to go? Is there someplace on your street you've passed numerous times that you can explore today? Go do it! Gold Star!

"If the stars should appear but one night every thousand years, how man would marvel and stare."

—RALPH WALDO EMERSON

Write a list of the most beautiful things you saw today:

GOOD DEED STARS

"It was only a sunny smile, and
little it cost in the giving, but
like morning light it scattered
the night and made the day
worth living."

—F. SCOTT FITZGERALD

Gold Stars all around for the small and big things you do for others and the planet! Did you compliment a friend today? Pet a cat? Give something away to charity? When you do good deeds, the world becomes shiny and bright.

Did you take the time to...

Clean out your closet and give things away: that old coat, fedora, or set of golf clubs? Gold Star!

Give someone flowers? Gold Star!

Let someone pull in front of you in traffic? Gold Star!

Make a snowman, leaf mosaic, or stone sculpture for others to see and enjoy? Gold Star!

Pay for the person behind you in line (a bridge toll, cup of coffee, movie ticket, bowl of ramen)? Gold Star!

Make someone laugh? Gold Star!

 Tell someone something you love about them?
Gold Star!

 Deliver soup to a friend who needs comfort (or is
just hungry)? Gold Star!

 Introduce two people who could help each other?
Gold Star!

 Show your mother how to use the latest cool app or
teach a child how to use chopsticks? Gold Star!

★ Do something for someone else without being asked. Extra credit: Do something for someone else and don't tell him/her. Gold Star!

Act of kindness: _____

☆ For: _____

Act of kindness: _____

☆ For: _____

Act of kindness: _____

☆ For: _____

Act of kindness: _____

☆ For: _____

Act of kindness: _____

☆ For: _____

Act of kindness:

☆ For:

Act of kindness:

☆ For:

Act of kindness:

☆ For:

Act of kindness:

☆ For:

Act of kindness:

☆ For:

Act of kindness:

☆ For:

What volunteer opportunities would benefit your community?
Write them down and commit to volunteering once a month.

Gather together a group of friends and clean up litter in your neighborhood or along the highway. Write down a list of projects and people to help complete them! Gold Stars for all!

☆ _____

☆ _____

☆ _____

☆ _____

☆ _____

☆ _____

☆ _____

Is there one thing you can do today to make a difference?

_____

_____

_____

_____

_____

_____

_____

Is there one thing you can do today to help a friend?

_____

_____

_____

_____

_____

_____

_____

Good Deeds:

_____

_____

_____

_____

_____

_____

_____

_____

_____

_____

_____

_____

_____

_____

GIVE SOMEONE
A GOLD STAR

"Appreciation is a wonderful thing
and it makes what is excellent in
others belong to us all."

—VOLTAIRE

Everyone loves a Gold Star! When you acknowledge others, you acknowledge that everyone and everything matters. We are all a part of the big, starry universe and can make the world a happy place for each other. So give some friends some Gold Stars!

Gold Star Support

Help someone get to the finish line—whether it was literally in a race, towards an ideal physical state, or on a project? Give them a Gold Star!

Start a cooking club, knitting circle, bowling league, or some kind of gathering group? Give your friends Gold Stars for showing up!

Teach a friend a new skill, like how to hang glide or play poker? Give them a Gold Star!

Give a friend a Gold Star just for being a good friend. Gold Star!

★ Honor someone's courage. In history, Gold Stars have had another meaning—they were displayed to indicate that a family member was lost in service. Take a moment to reflect on the contributions of others.

Create a Gold Star community (galaxy)

and take on a project. A group of stargazers

can change the world.

"For my part, I know nothing with any certainty, but the sight of the stars makes me dream."

—VINCENT VAN GOGH

Write down a list of five friends or family members who are working hard on something and send them a note with a big Gold Star for effort!

1.

2.

3.

4.

5.

Attend a friend's special event

(art exhibit, badminton tournament, sing-along festival)

and give them a Gold Star!

★ **Say it out loud!** When you achieve a Gold Star, it feels good to yell it out! See someone else accomplish one of their goals? Acknowledge them with an exuberant shout of "Gold Star!"

_____

_____

_____

_____

_____

_____

_____

_____

_____

_____

_____

_____

Think about the people on your all-star team and write down all the Gold Star things they do.

Person:

Gold Star Qualities:

Person:

Gold Star Qualities:

Person:

Gold Star Qualities:

Person:

Gold Star Qualities:

"What you get by achieving your goal is not as important as who you become by achieving your goals."

—HENRY DAVID THOREAU

SUPER STARS!

"Every great dream begins with a
dreamer. Always remember that
you have with you the strength, the
patience, and the passion to reach
for the stars to change the world."

—HARRIET TUBMAN

Super stars are for dreaming big and achieving our biggest goals. These stars are for the big moments that mean the most. Whatever your hopes and dreams are, write them down and make them happen! Go for the Super Stars because you are a superstar!

Imagine...

 What is your dream job? Do you want to launch a company? Write about it. Gold Star!

 What would be your dream house? Start a clipping file with ideas. Glue-stick a few clippings into this book. Gold Star!

 Can you make the world a better place? Volunteer. Gold Star!

Are you ready to get in shape? Choose a sport and start training. Gold Star!

 Do you want to see the world? Mark on a map or globe where you'd like to go. Gold Star!

 Do you want to create something? Construct a life-sized mobile? Paint a masterpiece? Explore the possibilities. Gold Star!

Write a list of your biggest dreams. What's on your bucket list? Is your dream to study polar bears in the North Pole or to surf with dolphins? Have you always wanted to dance in a parade?

"To be a star, you must shine your own light, follow your own path and don't worry about the darkness for that is when the stars shine the brightest."

—NAPOLEON HILL

"It is not in the stars to hold our destiny but in ourselves."

—WILLIAM SHAKESPEARE

What is your superstar? Can you write down what it might take to reach your goal?

Notes

Notes

ISBN 978-1-4521-3846-6

Manufactured in China

MIX
Paper from responsible sources
FSC™ C017606

Design by Sally Carmichael
Typeset in Arquitecta and Galicya Solid

Quotation Credits

Page 56: From *Selected Political Writings* by Mahatma Gandhi. Cambridge: Hackett Publishing, 1996. Reprinted with permission of Navaji Van Trust.

Page 6: From "Lunch with Rufus Wainwright" by Tom Lamont, published in The Guardian on April 21, 2012. Reproduced with permission of The Guardian.

Page 5: Copyright © Carl Sagan, 1973. From *The Cosmic Connection: An Extraterrestrial Perspective* by Carl Sagan. New York: Cambridge University Press, 2000. Originally published by Doubleday in 1973.

Chronicle Books publishes distinctive books and gifts. From award-winning children's titles, bestselling cookbooks, and eclectic pop culture to acclaimed works of art and design, stationery, and journals, we craft publishing that's instantly recognizable for its spirit and creativity. Enjoy our publishing and become part of our community at www.chroniclebooks.com.

10 9 8 7 6 5 4 3 2 1

Chronicle Books LLC
680 Second Street
San Francisco, CA 94107
www.chroniclebooks.com